2000 StiCKeRS

BIBLE STORIES

Favorite tales and 36 activities!

PaRRagon

Bath • New York • Cologne • Melbourne • Delhi
Hong Kong • Shenzhen • Singapore • Amsterdam

W9-BCA-826

Creation

God created the world.
Add more stars and plants.

Doodle some waves in the sea.

Animals

God made animals to live on the Earth.
Fill the scene with different creatures.

Adam and Eve

Adam and Eve were the first people.
Add more plants and animals
to the garden they lived in.

Noah's Ark

God told Noah to build an ark for the animals. Add more animals, so that there are two of each!

The Flood

It rained for 40 days and 40 nights.
Draw lots of raindrops in the sky.

Noah sent a dove to look for land.
Help the dove find its way.

5 days MAY

START

FINISH

Answer:

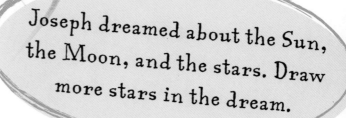

Joseph dreamed about the Sun, the Moon, and the stars. Draw more stars in the dream.

15 days

Decorate Joseph's blanket!

Joseph and the Pharaoh

Joseph helped the Pharaoh and became an important man in Egypt.

Add more jewels to Pharaoh's throne.

Draw the right gem to complete each necklace.

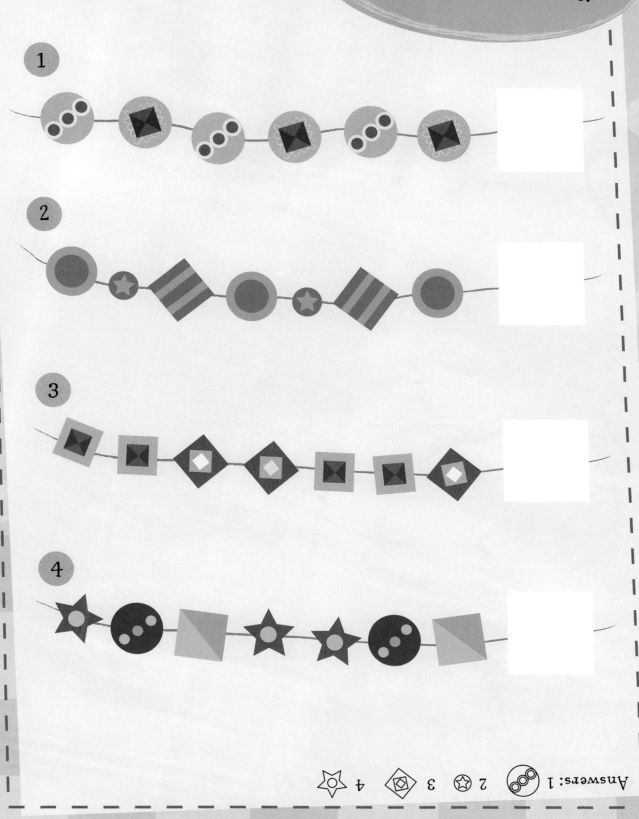

1

2

3

4

Answers: 1 ⊚ 2 ☆ 3 ◈ 4 ☆

Moses

An Egyptian princess
found Moses in a basket.
Which line leads to baby Moses?

A

B

C

Add more flowers
on the riverbank and
swimming ducks.

Plague of Frogs

God sent a plague of frogs to Egypt.
Add more frogs all over the scene.

The Red Sea

When Moses and his people left Egypt, the Red Sea parted to let them go. Add more people and Egyptian chariots.

How many
starfish can
you find?

Answer: There are 10 starfish.

Strong Samson

Samson was stronger than a whole army.
Draw what he is lifting.

Add lots of soldiers
to the army.

David and Goliath

David was a shepherd.
Add some more sheep to his field.

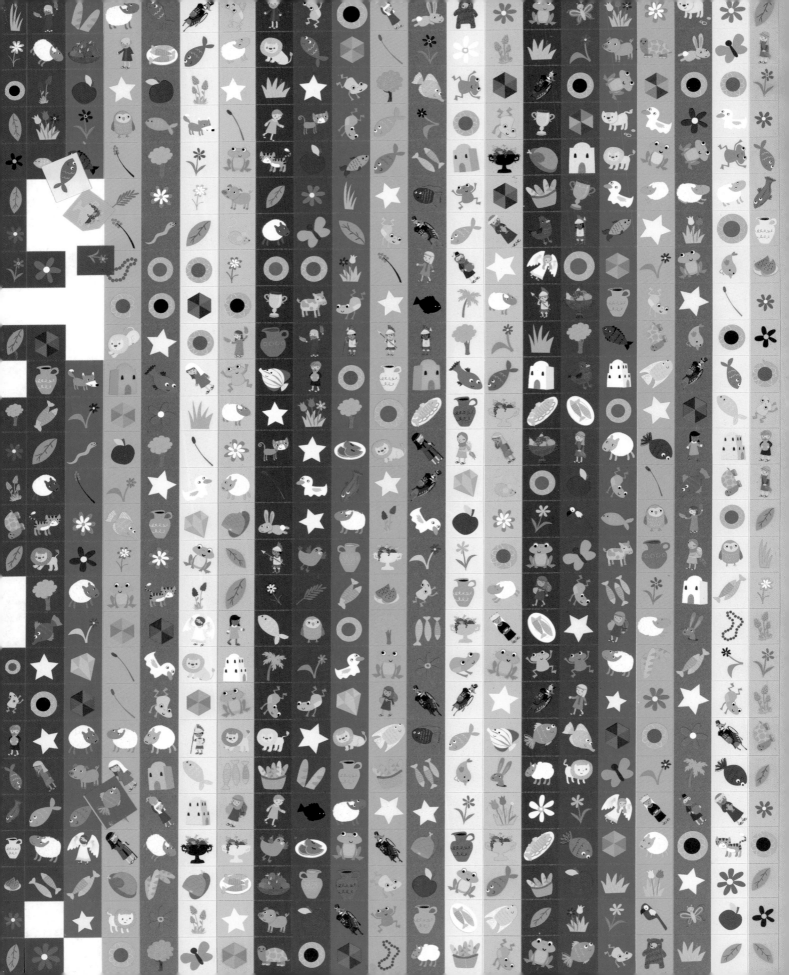

David used his slingshot to defeat Goliath. Decorate Goliath's armor and shield

Daniel

Daniel was thrown
into the lions' den,
but God saved him.
Add more lions.

How many mice
can you see?

Answer: There are 5 mice.

Jonah and the Big Fish

Jonah was swallowed by a big fish.
Copy the picture of it, using the grid to help you.

Add some more fish
in the water.

Mary and Joseph

The angel Gabriel told Mary
she would have a baby.

A

B

C

Which picture
matches Mary?

Connect the dots to finish the angel's wings.

Bethlehem

There was no room at the inn for
Mary and Joseph. Add more houses
and people to the scene.

Answer: Innkeeper C is different.

The Birth of Jesus

Jesus was born in a stable.
Complete the nativity scene!

Add shepherds, lambs, angels, and three wise men.

The Disciples

Jesus had 12 followers called disciples.
Complete the pattern on each disciple's robe.

Jesus's First Miracle

At a wedding, Jesus turned water into wine.

Decorate the wedding canopy!

Add more pitchers and some food to eat.

Feeding the 5000

Jesus turned five loaves and two fish into food for 5000 people.

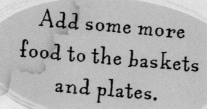

Add some more food to the baskets and plates.

The Good Samaritan

Jesus told a story about a Good Samaritan
who helped a traveler in trouble.

Find three robbers
hiding in the rocks.

Help the Good Samaritan find the traveler.

START

FINISH

Answer:

The Lost Son

A father held a huge feast for his son,
who had returned from a far-off town.

Can you find
the lost son in
the crowd?

Add more food to
the feast.

Jerusalem

Jesus rode into Jerusalem on the back of a donkey. Add more people and palm leaves.

The Last Supper

Jesus invited his disciples to the Last Supper.
Find five differences between the two pictures.

Answers: Brown pitcher, loaves of bread, one plate, missing disciple, blue robe.